MASTERING PRODUCTIVITY: 7 JAPANESE TECHNIQUES TO OVERCOME LAZINESS

Bill Galveston

CONTENTS

Title Page
Introduction: Overcoming Laziness for a Productive Life — 1
Chapter 1: Kaizen - Continuous Improvement: A Path to Overcoming Laziness — 8
Chapter 2: Ikigai - Finding Purpose: Igniting Your Inner Drive — 18
Chapter 3: Pomodoro Technique - Mastering Time Management for Laser Focus — 29
Chapter 4: Shoshin - Embracing the Beginner's Mind — 39
Chapter 5: Gaman - Harnessing Perseverance and Endurance for Success — 49
Chapter 6: Kaizen Mindset - Embracing Change for Continuous Improvement — 60
Chapter 7: Wabi-Sabi - Embracing Imperfection for Self-Acceptance and Authenticity — 71
Conclusion: Embrace the Wisdom of Japanese Techniques to Overcome Laziness — 81
Appendix: Resources for Further Exploration — 85
Glossary of Japanese Terms — 87

INTRODUCTION: OVERCOMING LAZINESS FOR A PRODUCTIVE LIFE

In today's fast-paced world, the struggle with laziness is a common challenge that many individuals face. Laziness, often characterized by procrastination, lack of motivation, and a sense of inertia, can hinder personal growth, professional success, and overall well-being. The desire to be productive and achieve our goals often clashes with the comfort of staying within our comfort zones. However, there is hope – and inspiration can be drawn from the wisdom of Japanese culture, which emphasizes discipline, dedication, and continuous improvement.

At its core, laziness is not simply a lack of action; it is a state of mind that can hold us back from reaching our full potential. Whether it's putting off tasks until the last minute, delaying important decisions, or avoiding responsibilities altogether, the consequences of succumbing to laziness can be detrimental to our goals, dreams, and aspirations.

The impact of laziness is not limited to our personal lives; it can seep into our professional endeavors as well. Missed deadlines, decreased productivity, and a lack of innovation can all be traced back to the habit of procrastination. The good news is that with the right mindset and strategies, laziness can be overcome.

In this ebook, we will delve into the rich landscape of Japanese culture to explore seven powerful techniques that can help you overcome laziness and cultivate a productive lifestyle. These techniques are deeply rooted in Japan's philosophy of discipline, purpose, and continuous improvement. By integrating these principles into your daily routine, you can break free from the chains of laziness and embark on a journey of self-transformation.

Each chapter of this ebook will focus on a specific Japanese technique and provide practical insights, actionable steps, and real-life examples of individuals who have successfully conquered their own tendencies toward laziness. As you read through these chapters, remember that change is a gradual process, and it requires dedication and consistent effort. By embracing the wisdom of Japan's cultural traditions, you can unlock your true potential and lead a life marked by accomplishment, fulfillment, and meaningful progress.

In the following chapters, we will explore the following techniques:

1. **Kaizen - Continuous Improvement:** Discover the power of small, incremental changes in overcoming laziness.

2. **Ikigai - Finding Purpose:** Uncover your passions and mission to infuse your life with purpose and drive.

3. **Pomodoro Technique - Time Management:** Harness-focused intervals to enhance productivity and combat procrastination.

4. **Shoshin - Embracing the Beginner's Mind:** Learn the art of approaching tasks with the wonder and curiosity of a

beginner to enhance concentration and efficiency.

5. **Gaman - Perseverance and Endurance:** Cultivate resilience to overcome challenges and stay motivated.

6. **Kaizen Mindset - Embracing Change:** Adopt a mindset of continuous improvement to break free from complacency.

7. **Wabi-Sabi - Embracing Imperfection:** Embrace imperfection and release the need for perfectionism to boost creativity.

As we journey through these techniques together, remember that transformation is a process that requires patience and self-compassion. The journey to overcome laziness is an investment in your future self – a self that is proactive, purpose-driven, and consistently strives for growth. Let's begin this journey toward a more productive and fulfilling life, drawing inspiration from the timeless wisdom of Japanese culture.

The Importance of Productivity: Fueling Your Path to Achievement

In the pursuit of our dreams and aspirations, productivity stands as a cornerstone that can make the difference between success and stagnation. While the concept of productivity might conjure images of busy schedules and endless to-do lists, it encompasses so much more than just the quantity of tasks completed. Productivity is about efficiently channeling your energy, time, and resources to achieve meaningful goals, enabling you to create a life that aligns with your deepest desires.

1. Turning Dreams into Reality:
Imagine having a clear vision of your goals, backed by a plan of action that propels you forward. Productivity transforms mere wishes into tangible realities. Whether your ambition is to write a novel, launch a business, learn a new language, or adopt

a healthier lifestyle, being productive empowers you to take consistent steps toward your objectives. Every small effort adds up over time, accumulating into significant progress.

2. Maximizing Your Potential:
Human potential is vast and limitless, but it can remain dormant without the spark of productivity. When you harness your time effectively, you tap into your inherent capacity for growth, creativity, and innovation. Productivity encourages you to explore new horizons, develop new skills, and push beyond your comfort zones. By unlocking your potential, you open doors to opportunities you might have never imagined.

3. Fostering a Sense of Fulfillment:
The satisfaction derived from accomplishing goals extends far beyond the completion of tasks. Productivity generates a profound sense of fulfillment and achievement. It validates your efforts and provides a sense of purpose and direction. When you consistently make progress, you experience a deep sense of satisfaction that boosts your confidence and self-esteem.

4. Overcoming Procrastination and Laziness:
Laziness and procrastination can act as formidable barriers on your path to success. Productivity is the antidote to these obstacles. It empowers you to break free from the grip of inertia and tackle tasks head-on. By taking purposeful actions, you diminish the influence of laziness and create momentum that propels you forward.

5. Crafting a Balanced Life:
Productivity is not solely about work-related tasks; it extends to all aspects of your life. By efficiently managing your time and commitments, you can strike a balance between your personal, professional, and leisure pursuits. This equilibrium is essential for maintaining your overall well-being and preventing burnout.

6. Creating Lasting Impact:
Productivity often involves the completion of projects that leave

a mark on the world. Whether you're creating art, contributing to your community, or making advancements in your field, the outcomes of your productive efforts can have a lasting impact on others and the world at large.

As you embark on the journey of overcoming laziness through the Japanese techniques outlined in this ebook, keep in mind that productivity is not an end in itself; it's a means to an end – the end being a life that resonates with purpose, accomplishment, and growth. By nurturing your productivity, you unlock the door to your fullest potential and set the stage for a journey of continuous improvement. Remember, the steps you take today are the building blocks of the future you're crafting, one productive moment at a time.

Cultural Influence of Japan: A Legacy of Productivity and Self-Discipline

When it comes to productivity and self-discipline, few cultures have left as indelible a mark as Japan. Rooted in centuries of tradition and philosophy, the Japanese approach to these concepts has not only shaped the nation's success but has also become a source of inspiration for people around the world seeking to enhance their own lives. The cultural influence of Japan in the field of productivity and self-discipline is a testament to the profound impact that cultural values can have on shaping individual behavior and societal norms.

1. Embracing Diligence and Craftsmanship:
Japan's cultural heritage is deeply intertwined with craftsmanship and attention to detail. The meticulous approach to creating everything from traditional tea ceremonies to intricate artworks has cultivated a sense of dedication and diligence. This mindset extends to everyday tasks, emphasizing the value of giving one's best effort, regardless of the task's scale. This commitment to excellence has driven the Japanese to

approach their work with a sense of purpose and pride, setting a benchmark for productivity.

2. Incorporating Ritual and Routine:
Japanese culture places a strong emphasis on rituals and routines, which create a sense of structure and discipline. From morning rituals to the practice of mindfulness, these routines instill a sense of order and intention in daily life. These practices not only enhance productivity but also promote mental clarity and a focused mindset. By adhering to these routines, the Japanese have demonstrated how consistency and discipline can lead to increased efficiency.

3. Commitment to Continuous Improvement:
The concept of "Kaizen," meaning continuous improvement, is a cornerstone of Japanese philosophy. This principle encourages individuals to make small, incremental changes over time, leading to significant growth. The emphasis on Kaizen has fostered a culture of lifelong learning and self-improvement. By applying this philosophy to personal and professional endeavors, the Japanese have showcased how the pursuit of growth can be a powerful motivator in combating laziness and complacency.

4. Honoring Tradition and Legacy:
Japanese culture values tradition and heritage, emphasizing the importance of honoring the past while moving forward. This respect for tradition is balanced with an openness to innovation and change, creating a unique blend of stability and adaptability. By valuing both the old and the new, the Japanese have cultivated a mindset that embraces growth and productivity without losing sight of their cultural roots.

5. Mindfulness and Present-Moment Awareness:
The practice of mindfulness, often found in Japanese cultural activities such as tea ceremonies and Zen meditation, encourages individuals to be fully present in the moment. This awareness enhances focus and concentration, enabling people to overcome

distractions and approach tasks with clarity and intention. Mindfulness has become an integral tool in combating laziness by grounding individuals in the present and minimizing the allure of procrastination.

In the pages that follow, we will explore seven Japanese techniques that draw from this rich cultural heritage. These techniques offer practical guidance on overcoming laziness, increasing productivity, and embracing a purpose-driven life. By integrating these principles into your daily routine, you'll tap into the wisdom of a culture that has long understood the transformative power of discipline, mindfulness, and continuous improvement. As you embark on this journey, remember that the cultural influence of Japan serves as a guiding light, illuminating a path toward a more productive and fulfilled existence.

CHAPTER 1: KAIZEN – CONTINUOUS IMPROVEMENT: A PATH TO OVERCOMING LAZINESS

In a world that often demands instant results, the Japanese philosophy of Kaizen stands as a refreshing approach to personal growth and productivity. Rooted in the belief that consistent, incremental changes lead to significant improvement over time, Kaizen offers a powerful strategy to overcome laziness and embrace continuous progress.

Origins of Kaizen in Japanese Culture:

The term "Kaizen" derives from two Japanese words: "kai," meaning change, and "zen," signifying good. Together, they encapsulate the idea of making positive changes for improvement. Kaizen finds its roots in post-World War II Japan when the nation was rebuilding its economy. Faced with limited resources, Japanese industries and businesses turned to Kaizen as a means of improving efficiency and quality. This approach allowed them to create substantial advancements through small, manageable steps.

However, Kaizen's influence extends beyond the realm of business. The concept embodies a holistic philosophy that emphasizes the pursuit of continuous self-improvement in every aspect of life. From personal habits to professional endeavors, Kaizen provides a framework for breaking down goals into manageable components and making consistent progress.

The Essence of Kaizen:

At the heart of Kaizen lies the recognition that monumental changes often stem from minor adjustments. This perspective contrasts with the idea that success requires massive overhauls or grand gestures. Instead, Kaizen encourages individuals to focus on the present moment and take small, actionable steps that are sustainable over time.

Kaizen operates on several key principles:

1. **Start Small:** Kaizen recognizes that change can be daunting, leading to resistance and procrastination. By starting with tiny, achievable steps, individuals can overcome the inertia of laziness and build momentum.

2. **Consistency:** The power of Kaizen lies in its consistency. Regular, incremental improvements compound over time to create significant transformation. This consistency reduces the overwhelming nature of big changes and enables long-lasting habits.

3. **Self-Reflection:** Kaizen promotes self-awareness and reflection. By evaluating the outcomes of small changes, individuals can make informed adjustments, refining their strategies for greater effectiveness.

4. **Continuous Learning:** A Kaizen mindset embraces a love of learning. It encourages individuals to seek new knowledge, experiment with different approaches, and remain open to innovation.

5. **Embracing Mistakes:** Kaizen fosters an environment where mistakes are seen as opportunities for growth, not failures. This perspective minimizes the fear of failure that often contributes to laziness and inaction.

Applying Kaizen to Overcome Laziness: A Journey of Small Steps:

The Kaizen philosophy can be a powerful tool in conquering laziness and procrastination. By focusing on small, manageable changes, individuals can sidestep the overwhelm that often accompanies ambitious goals. Instead of facing an insurmountable task, they break it down into smaller, achievable steps, making progress more attainable and engaging.

Laziness often stems from a sense of overwhelm, a lack of motivation, or the allure of comfort. The principle of Kaizen offers a powerful antidote to these barriers, providing a structured and effective approach to conquer laziness and ignite a drive for continuous improvement. By embracing Kaizen, you can transform your relationship with productivity and embark on a journey of gradual, sustainable change.

1. Set Micro-Goals:
Kaizen encourages you to start with micro-goals, which are tiny, manageable tasks that align with your larger objectives. When faced with a project that seems daunting, breaking it into smaller, achievable steps can eliminate the sense of paralysis that laziness often brings. Whether it's reading a single page of a book, writing a paragraph, or taking a ten-minute walk, these micro-goals build a bridge between inaction and progress.

2. Celebrate Mini-Wins:

Incorporating Kaizen means celebrating even the smallest victories. Each micro-goal you accomplish should be acknowledged as a triumph, boosting your motivation and creating a positive feedback loop. This celebration of progress cultivates a sense of achievement, counteracting the inertia of laziness and motivating you to keep moving forward.

3. Build Consistency:
Consistency is the cornerstone of Kaizen. By committing to consistent action, you establish a routine that gradually replaces laziness with a sense of purpose and discipline. Whether it's dedicating a specific time each day to work on a task or setting a weekly goal, the act of consistently showing up chips away at the resistance to getting started.

4. Embrace Imperfection:
One of the most significant hurdles to productivity is the pursuit of perfection. Kaizen teaches us that perfection isn't the goal; progress is. Embrace the idea that imperfection is part of the journey and that mistakes are stepping stones to improvement. This perspective minimizes the fear of failure that often contributes to laziness and empowers you to take action.

5. Reflect and Adjust:
Regular self-reflection is a key element of Kaizen. Periodically evaluate your progress and assess whether your micro-goals are driving you toward your desired outcome. If something isn't working, adjust your approach. This self-awareness ensures that you remain engaged and motivated, preventing stagnation and the return of laziness.

6. Gradual Expansion:
As you become comfortable with the Kaizen approach, gradually expand your micro-goals. The process of increasing the complexity of tasks mirrors your growth, allowing you to tackle more significant challenges over time. This progression is a testament to your dedication and an effective countermeasure to

laziness.

7. Savor the Journey:
The Kaizen mindset encourages you to focus on the journey rather than fixating solely on the destination. Savoring each step and finding joy in the process counteracts the sense of drudgery that laziness often brings. By cultivating a positive attitude toward your efforts, you create an environment where productivity thrives.

Incorporating Kaizen into your life requires patience and a commitment to consistent, incremental progress. It's about recognizing that the path to overcoming laziness is paved with small steps, each contributing to your growth and transformation. By adopting this approach, you shift your mindset from inaction to action, infusing your days with purpose, accomplishment, and a sense of purposeful momentum.

Practical Steps for Incorporating Small, Incremental Changes in Daily Routines

Incorporating the principles of Kaizen into your daily life involves making small, gradual adjustments that accumulate over time, leading to significant improvements. By adopting these practical steps, you can effectively overcome laziness and create a path towards sustained growth and productivity.

1. Identify Specific Areas for Improvement:
Start by identifying areas of your life where you want to make changes. Whether it's related to health, work, learning, or personal habits, pinpointing specific aspects will give your efforts direction and purpose.

2. Set Micro-Goals:
Break down your goals into micro-goals – tiny tasks that are easy to accomplish. These micro-goals should be so simple that you'll find it hard to say no to them. For instance, if you want to read

more, commit to reading a single page each day.

3. Establish a Routine:
Consistency is key to Kaizen. Integrate your micro-goals into your daily routine, making them a non-negotiable part of your day. Whether it's allocating a certain time in the morning or during breaks, create a dedicated slot for your incremental changes.

4. Start with a Tiny Commitment:
The initial step should be effortless to the point that it feels almost automatic. For example, if you want to start exercising, commit to doing a single push-up or stretching for a minute. This minimal commitment reduces the resistance associated with laziness.

5. Track Your Progress:
Create a visual tracker or journal to record your daily achievements. Seeing your progress build over time can be highly motivating and help reinforce your commitment to the small changes you're making.

6. Use Triggers:
Associate your micro-goals with existing habits or triggers. For example, if you want to drink more water, make it a rule to have a glass of water every time you make a cup of tea or coffee.

7. Increase Gradually:
As you build consistency and confidence, gradually increase the complexity or intensity of your micro-goals. The key is to challenge yourself without overwhelming your capacity for change.

8. Celebrate Small Wins:
Each accomplishment, no matter how minor, deserves celebration. This positive reinforcement strengthens the connection between action and reward, making you more likely to continue your efforts.

9. Reflect and Adjust Regularly:
Set aside time to reflect on your progress. Are the changes you're

making effective? Do you need to adjust your micro-goals? Adapt your approach based on your observations to optimize your efforts.

10. Stay Patient and Persistent:
Kaizen is about the journey, not the destination. Understand that change takes time and effort. The key is persistence – even on days when you're struggling, showing up and making that tiny effort counts.

11. Build a Support System:
Share your Kaizen journey with friends, family, or a supportive community. Having accountability partners can provide encouragement and motivation, especially when faced with moments of laziness.

By consistently applying these practical steps, you'll gradually shift your mindset away from laziness and toward a proactive, growth-oriented approach. Over time, the small, incremental changes you make will accumulate, resulting in profound transformations that will enrich your personal and professional life. Remember, the journey of a thousand miles begins with a single step – and Kaizen ensures that each step is purposeful and effective.

Real-Life Examples of Kaizen Transformations:

1. The Reading Habit Reinvented:
Samantha, an avid reader, wanted to read more non-fiction books to expand her knowledge. She struggled with procrastination and often found herself putting off reading due to its perceived time commitment. Applying Kaizen, Samantha committed to reading just one page of a non-fiction book each day. Over time, this small change not only made reading feel less overwhelming but also led to the completion of multiple books she might have otherwise delayed reading.

2. Fitness Journey Reimagined:

Mark had a goal to incorporate regular exercise into his busy schedule. He struggled with finding time and motivation to work out consistently. Applying Kaizen, he started with a micro-goal of doing five push-ups every morning. As these five push-ups became a habit, he gradually increased the number. Over the course of several months, Mark went from five to twenty push-ups and eventually established a full exercise routine that he maintained with ease.

3. Language Learning Success:

Amanda had always wanted to learn a new language but found the task daunting. Applying Kaizen, she began by dedicating just five minutes each day to practicing vocabulary and phrases. With time, this small daily effort became an integral part of her routine. Over the course of a year, Amanda's consistency resulted in significant language proficiency and the ability to hold conversations in the new language.

4. Professional Growth with Kaizen:

John, a project manager, struggled with time management and organization. He often felt overwhelmed by his workload and procrastinated on important tasks. John adopted Kaizen by setting a micro-goal of spending ten minutes each morning organizing his tasks for the day. This small investment of time allowed him to approach his work with clarity and focus, leading to increased productivity and a sense of accomplishment.

5. Artistic Pursuits Redefined:

Emily had a passion for painting but frequently found herself delaying creative projects due to laziness and self-doubt. With Kaizen, she committed to spending just five minutes every evening sketching or painting. Over time, her small daily efforts not only improved her skills but also reignited her enthusiasm for art. This commitment eventually led to the creation of a portfolio that she proudly shared with others.

6. Healthy Eating Habits Established:

Sarah struggled to maintain a healthy diet due to her busy lifestyle and tendency to opt for convenience foods. She decided to apply Kaizen by incorporating one serving of fruits or vegetables into one meal each day. This small change gradually expanded her palate and led to healthier eating habits. Over time, Sarah found herself naturally making better food choices and feeling more energized.

7. Writing Dreams Achieved:

Jacob aspired to write a book, but he frequently succumbed to writer's block and procrastination. Applying Kaizen, he committed to writing just fifty words every day. This minimal effort removed the pressure of creating lengthy content and allowed him to make consistent progress. Over the course of a year, Jacob had written a significant portion of his book, proving that even the smallest daily contributions can lead to substantial accomplishments.

8. Digital Detox Success:

Julia wanted to reduce her screen time and increase her mindfulness. She decided to apply Kaizen by designating the first five minutes after waking up and the last five minutes before sleeping as screen-free periods. This micro-goal allowed her to start and end her day with intention, leading to improved focus and a more restful sleep.

9. Financial Discipline Attained:

Mike struggled with impulse spending and wanted to improve his financial habits. He implemented Kaizen by setting a micro-goal to save a small amount of money every day. This change gradually transformed his spending behavior, and he found himself more mindful of his purchases. Over time, Mike's consistent savings built financial security and discipline.

10. Household Organization Triumph:

Alexis aimed to declutter and organize her living space but felt overwhelmed by the task. Using Kaizen, she committed to dedicating just fifteen minutes each day to decluttering one area of her home. Over several weeks, her living space transformed from chaotic to orderly. The gradual approach not only eliminated the stress of a massive cleaning spree but also cultivated a sense of accomplishment.

These real-life examples highlight how Kaizen can transform lives by starting with tiny, manageable steps. By breaking down goals and consistently making incremental changes, these individuals overcame their initial inertia and achieved meaningful progress. The Kaizen approach illustrates that even the smallest actions can accumulate into significant achievements, proving that laziness can be defeated with persistence, purpose, and the power of continuous improvement.

CHAPTER 2: IKIGAI - FINDING PURPOSE: IGNITING YOUR INNER DRIVE

In a world often dominated by the pursuit of success and material gain, the Japanese concept of Ikigai provides a profound perspective on living a fulfilled and purpose-driven life. Rooted in centuries of wisdom, Ikigai offers a holistic approach that goes beyond mere productivity, encouraging us to explore the intersection of passion, mission, vocation, and profession. This chapter delves into the concept of Ikigai, its origins, and its transformative potential in overcoming laziness and igniting a sense of purpose.

Origins of Ikigai in Japanese Philosophy:

The term "Ikigai" combines two Japanese words: "iki," meaning life, and "gai," meaning value or worth. Together, they encapsulate the idea of finding value and meaning in one's life. Ikigai originated on the Japanese island of Okinawa, known for its high concentration of centenarians and vibrant, healthy lifestyles.

This concept has since transcended geographical boundaries and cultural barriers, resonating with individuals worldwide seeking deeper meaning in their existence.

The Significance of Ikigai:

At its core, Ikigai is a powerful framework that encourages individuals to explore their passions, align their efforts with their inner values, and find a sense of purpose in their daily activities. This philosophy suggests that the sweet spot where passion, mission, vocation, and profession intersect is where true fulfillment and satisfaction lie.

1. Passion:
Ikigai invites you to discover what brings you joy and excitement. This could be a hobby, activity, or interest that energizes you and makes time fly. Passion is the driving force that fuels your sense of purpose.

2. Mission:
Finding your mission involves identifying how you can contribute to the world, your community, or the lives of others. It's about understanding how your unique strengths and qualities can make a positive impact.

3. Vocation:
Vocation refers to what you're good at – your skills and talents. It's what you can offer to the world in a practical sense. Discovering your vocation involves recognizing your natural abilities and the areas where you excel.

4. Profession:
Profession is the practical aspect of Ikigai – it's how you make a living. While it's important, it's just one piece of the puzzle. Aligning your profession with your passion, mission, and vocation can lead to a sense of purposeful work.

5. The Harmony of Ikigai:
The essence of Ikigai lies in the harmony created when these four

elements intersect. When you engage in activities that fulfill all these aspects, you're likely to experience a deep sense of purpose, satisfaction, and even joy. It's in this state that laziness loses its grip, and you're motivated by the inherent value and meaning in what you do.

Applying Ikigai to Overcome Laziness:

Ikigai provides a profound antidote to laziness by encouraging you to tap into the wellspring of motivation that comes from living a life aligned with your passions and values. By discovering your unique Ikigai, you can transcend the inertia of laziness and infuse your days with purpose and intention. This chapter will guide you through the process of uncovering your Ikigai and embracing it as a powerful force for transformation.

Harnessing Ikigai to Combat Laziness: A Multi-Faceted Approach

Identifying one's passion, mission, vocation, and profession through the lens of Ikigai presents a multi-faceted strategy for combating laziness and embracing a purpose-driven life. This approach addresses the root causes of laziness and offers a holistic solution that engages your mind, heart, and actions.

1. Passion: Igniting Inner Fire:
Passion is the spark that lights the fire of motivation within you. When you're passionate about something, laziness takes a backseat because your excitement propels you forward. Engaging in activities you're genuinely enthusiastic about eliminates the resistance that laziness often brings. Whether it's a hobby, creative pursuit, or any endeavor that brings you joy, passion fuels your eagerness to take action.

2. Mission: Cultivating a Sense of Responsibility:
Having a mission or purpose infuses your actions with a deeper sense of responsibility. When you recognize that your efforts

contribute to a greater cause or make a positive impact, laziness becomes incongruent with your values. The knowledge that you're working towards something meaningful compels you to overcome inertia and dedicate yourself to your mission.

3. Vocation: Capitalizing on Natural Abilities:
Discovering your vocation involves recognizing your inherent skills and talents. When you engage in activities that utilize your strengths, laziness loses its grip because you're operating in your zone of competence. The satisfaction that comes from excelling in what you do serves as a powerful motivator, propelling you to take action even when faced with challenges.

4. Profession: Aligning with Fulfillment:
A profession that aligns with your passion, mission, and vocation enhances your sense of fulfillment. When your work resonates with your values and strengths, you're less likely to succumb to laziness because your actions are directly connected to your personal and professional growth. A sense of purpose drives you to consistently invest effort in your chosen field.

5. Holistic Integration: Balancing the Quadrants:
The beauty of Ikigai lies in the harmonious integration of these four elements. Combating laziness becomes more effective when you're engaging in activities that encompass all facets of Ikigai. Each element complements the others, reinforcing your motivation and drive. The holistic nature of Ikigai ensures that you're addressing not only the external symptoms of laziness but also the internal factors that influence it.

6. Mindset Shift: From Drudgery to Meaningful Action:
By identifying your Ikigai, you shift your mindset from viewing tasks as burdensome to embracing them as meaningful endeavors. Laziness often thrives in the realm of the mundane and uninspiring. However, when you're actively pursuing your passions, fulfilling your mission, employing your natural talents, and engaging in fulfilling work, the concept of laziness becomes

incongruent with your purpose-driven life.

Incorporating Ikigai into your journey of combating laziness encourages a holistic transformation. By exploring and aligning your passion, mission, vocation, and profession, you craft a life that is inherently meaningful and engaging. This sense of purpose becomes your shield against the allure of laziness, propelling you towards sustained growth, accomplishment, and a fulfilling existence.

Exercises to Uncover Your Ikigai and Align Your Efforts:

1. Passion Exploration:

- Make a list of activities, hobbies, or interests that genuinely excite you.
- Reflect on moments when you felt most alive and engaged. What were you doing?
- Identify common themes or patterns in your passions to uncover areas that ignite your enthusiasm.

2. Mission Discovery:

- Consider the positive impact you want to have on others, your community, or the world.
- Reflect on the issues that resonate deeply with you and where you'd like to contribute.
- Imagine the legacy you'd like to leave behind and how you'd like to be remembered.

3. Vocation Reflection:

- List your natural talents, skills, and strengths.
- Reflect on tasks that come easily to you and activities you excel at.
- Consider how you can leverage your abilities to bring value to others or your chosen field.

4. Profession Alignment:

- Evaluate your current profession or career path.
- Reflect on how it aligns with your passion, mission, and vocation.
- Identify areas where you can make adjustments to better align your work with your Ikigai.

5. Ikigai Intersection:

- Create a Venn diagram with four overlapping circles representing passion, mission, vocation, and profession.
- In the overlapping areas, write down the activities or pursuits that fall into multiple categories.
- Explore how these intersections resonate with you and consider how they can guide your actions.

6. Vision Board Creation:

- Gather images, quotes, and symbols that represent your passions, values, and aspirations.
- Create a vision board that visually captures your Ikigai.
- Display the vision board where you'll see it daily to reinforce your alignment with your purpose.

7. Personal Values Assessment:

- Identify your core values – the principles that guide your choices and decisions.
- Reflect on how your passions, mission, vocation, and profession align with these values.
- Ensure that your pursuits are congruent with what matters most to you.

8. Small Actions Experiment:

- Choose a micro-goal related to your Ikigai, such as spending 10 minutes a day on a passion or volunteering.
- Dedicate consistent effort to this action and reflect on how it

affects your motivation and sense of purpose.

9. Journaling and Self-Reflection:

- Set aside regular time for introspection and journaling.
- Write about your passions, strengths, values, and areas where you find fulfillment.
- Use journaling as a tool to deepen your understanding of your Ikigai over time.

10. Seek Feedback from Others:

- Ask friends, family, or colleagues what they believe your strengths and passions are.
- Their insights can offer a fresh perspective and validate areas where you're aligned with your Ikigai.

Remember that uncovering your Ikigai is a journey, not an instant revelation. These exercises are designed to guide you through introspection and self-discovery. Be patient with yourself and embrace the process. As you align your efforts with your Ikigai, you'll find that the motivation to overcome laziness comes naturally, driven by a sense of purpose that fuels your actions.

Stories of Ikigai Transformations:

1. Embracing Creative Fulfillment:

Emily was stuck in a monotonous office job that left her feeling unfulfilled. Through self-reflection and exploration, she realized her passion for painting and storytelling. She decided to pursue a career as an illustrator, aligning her passion for art, her mission to inspire others through stories, and her natural talent for visual communication. As Emily dedicated herself to her newfound profession, her sense of purpose blossomed. She overcame laziness and procrastination by being driven to create meaningful art that resonated with others. Through her alignment with Ikigai, Emily transformed her life from one of routine to a journey of artistic fulfillment.

2. Healing and Empowerment Through Teaching:
After overcoming a personal health challenge, Mark discovered a deep passion for wellness and personal development. He realized that his mission was to help others lead healthier lives. Mark's vocation in education allowed him to combine his love for teaching with his newfound mission. He became a wellness coach, guiding individuals towards healthier choices. By aligning his profession with his Ikigai, Mark experienced a profound shift in his energy and motivation. His commitment to his mission propelled him to overcome laziness and dedicate himself to empowering others through education and positive lifestyle changes.

3. From Procrastination to Purposeful Entrepreneurship:
Sarah struggled with laziness and lacked motivation in her job as a marketing executive. Digging into her Ikigai, she discovered a passion for sustainable living, a mission to reduce environmental impact, and a vocation for creativity and problem-solving. She decided to start a business that offered eco-friendly products and solutions. Sarah's alignment with her Ikigai transformed her work ethic. The passion she felt for her business made it easy to overcome laziness, leading to the successful launch of her venture. By connecting her actions to a purpose greater than herself, Sarah experienced newfound drive and enthusiasm.

4. Inspiring Change Through Community Involvement:
John had always felt drawn to helping his community, but his demanding corporate job left him feeling disconnected from his values. As he explored his Ikigai, he realized his passion for community involvement and his vocation in leadership and organization. John began volunteering with local charities, organizing events, and mentoring youth. Through his alignment with his Ikigai, John's energy levels

surged. The sense of purpose he found in his activities enabled him to overcome laziness and dedicate himself to making a positive impact. John's transformation showcased the power of Ikigai in guiding him towards a life of service and fulfillment.

5. From Corporate Burnout to Holistic Wellness:

Jane had spent years climbing the corporate ladder, but the stress and burnout took a toll on her well-being. Through self-discovery, she uncovered her passion for holistic wellness, her mission to help others achieve balance, and her vocation in communication. Jane transitioned to a career as a wellness coach, aligning her profession with her Ikigai. As she guided clients towards better health and balance, her own sense of purpose flourished. Overcoming laziness became natural, driven by her commitment to nurturing others' well-being. Through her Ikigai, Jane transformed from a state of stress to a life of purposeful wellness.

6. Empowering Through Education:

Miguel grew up in a disadvantaged community and witnessed the impact of limited access to education. Through self-reflection, he identified his passion for education, his mission to empower underprivileged youth, and his vocation in teaching and mentorship. Miguel became a dedicated teacher, striving to provide quality education to his students. His alignment with his Ikigai fueled his motivation to overcome laziness and dedicate himself to preparing future generations for success. Through his teaching, Miguel was able to break cycles of disadvantage and uplift his community.

7. Rediscovering Joy Through Culinary Arts:

After years of working in a high-stress corporate environment, David found himself feeling disconnected and unfulfilled. He explored his Ikigai and realized his passion for cooking, his mission to create memorable experiences, and his vocation in creativity. David enrolled in culinary school and pursued a career as a chef. Through his alignment with his Ikigai, he transformed his life. Overcoming laziness was no longer a challenge; his love for cooking and the joy it brought him drove him to embrace every moment in the kitchen. David's story showcases how aligning with Ikigai can lead to a life rich in satisfaction and happiness.

8. Building Connection Through Art Therapy:

Rebecca always had a talent for art and a deep empathy for others. Through self-reflection, she uncovered her passion for creative expression, her mission to support mental well-being, and her vocation in artistic skills. Rebecca became an art therapist, using her creative abilities to help clients overcome challenges and heal. Her alignment with her Ikigai empowered her to overcome laziness, as her work was intrinsically meaningful and fulfilling. Through art therapy, Rebecca not only transformed her own life but also facilitated transformation in the lives of those she helped.

9. From Routine to Adventure:

Amanda had always followed a safe and predictable path, but she felt an emptiness within her. Through introspection, she realized her passion for travel, her mission to explore new cultures, and her vocation in storytelling. Amanda embarked on a journey of becoming a travel writer, aligning her profession with her Ikigai. The excitement of discovering new places and sharing her experiences with others fueled her motivation. Overcoming laziness became second nature, as every adventure was a step closer to fulfilling her Ikigai. Through her alignment with Ikigai, Amanda transformed her life from routine to a vibrant tapestry of exploration and purpose.

10. Tech Innovation for Social Change:

Alex, a software engineer, felt a disconnect between his job and his values. Through self-discovery, he identified his passion for technology, his mission to drive positive social change, and his vocation in problem-solving. Alex started a social enterprise, using technology to address pressing social issues. Aligning his profession with his Ikigai, he harnessed his skills for a greater purpose. The alignment empowered him to overcome laziness, as every line of code was a step towards his mission. Through his social enterprise, Alex showcased how Ikigai can infuse work with profound meaning and impact.

These stories exemplify the transformative power of Ikigai in individuals' lives. By aligning their passions, missions, vocations, and professions, these individuals harnessed a deep well of motivation and purpose. In doing so, they overcame laziness and embarked on paths of meaningful growth and accomplishment. The concept of Ikigai serves as a reminder that a life driven by purpose is a life rich with fulfillment, regardless of the challenges faced along the way.

CHAPTER 3: POMODORO TECHNIQUE - MASTERING TIME MANAGEMENT FOR LASER FOCUS

In a world characterized by constant distractions and the ever-present struggle against procrastination, the Pomodoro Technique emerges as a powerful tool for enhancing time management and boosting focus. Originating from the Italian word for "tomato," this technique is named after a kitchen timer shaped like a tomato, and it offers a structured approach to breaking down work into manageable intervals. This chapter dives into the Pomodoro Technique, unveiling its methodology and demonstrating how it effectively combats laziness while fostering increased productivity.

The Essence of the Pomodoro Technique:

At its core, the Pomodoro Technique revolves around the idea that focused work is most effective when done in short, concentrated bursts. This technique capitalizes on the brain's capacity for sustained attention within specific time frames, and it empowers individuals to harness that attention for optimal productivity. By breaking work into intervals and integrating short breaks, the Pomodoro Technique transforms work sessions from daunting stretches into manageable segments.

The Pomodoro Technique's Methodology:

1. **Set a Timer:** Choose a task to work on, set a timer for 25 minutes (traditionally referred to as a "Pomodoro"), and commit to working on that task without interruption during this interval.

2. **Engage in Deep Work:** Dive into your task with laser focus, utilizing the Pomodoro interval to immerse yourself in concentrated effort. The absence of distractions during this period enhances your work quality and efficiency.

3. **Embrace the Break:** Once the 25-minute Pomodoro is completed, reward yourself with a 5-minute break. Use this time to relax, stretch, or briefly detach from the task.

4. **Rinse and Repeat:** After four Pomodoros, take a longer break of 15-30 minutes. This extended break rejuvenates your energy and prepares you for the next work session.

Effectiveness in Combating Laziness:

The Pomodoro Technique addresses the psychological barriers that often lead to laziness:

- **Overwhelm:** By segmenting work into manageable intervals, the technique eliminates the sense of being overwhelmed by a large task, making it easier to get started.

- **Procrastination:** The Pomodoro Technique minimizes the

temptation to procrastinate by focusing your attention on a short, achievable timeframe. The countdown of the timer creates a sense of urgency that counteracts procrastination.

- **Distraction:** During Pomodoro intervals, distractions are intentionally put on hold. This commitment to focused work cultivates discipline, reducing the likelihood of succumbing to laziness induced by diversions.

- **Task Initiation:** Initiating work is often the hardest step. By committing to just 25 minutes of work, the barrier to starting is significantly lowered, encouraging action.

Enhancing Focus and Productivity:

The Pomodoro Technique enhances productivity by creating a rhythm of intense work followed by short, rejuvenating breaks. This rhythm prevents burnout, maintains a high level of focus, and sustains motivation throughout the workday. By adhering to this cycle, individuals can effectively manage their time, overcome laziness, and achieve higher levels of productivity.

Applying the Pomodoro Technique:

By integrating the Pomodoro Technique into your routine, you can transform your approach to work and overcome the inertia of laziness. This chapter guides you through the process of implementing the technique, providing practical strategies for breaking down tasks, managing time, and maximizing your output. Through the Pomodoro Technique, you'll unlock the potential to achieve more with focused, intentional effort while conquering the allure of laziness that often hampers progress.

Breaking Tasks into Focused Intervals: The Pomodoro Technique in Action

The process of breaking tasks into focused intervals, also known as Pomodoros, followed by short breaks is the cornerstone of the

Pomodoro Technique. This structured approach optimizes your focus and productivity while effectively combating the tendency to succumb to laziness and distractions. Here's a step-by-step guide to implementing this technique:

Step 1: Choose Your Task

Select a task that you want to work on. It could be anything from studying, writing, coding, cleaning, or any other task that requires your attention.

Step 2: Set the Timer

Set a timer for a standard Pomodoro interval, which is typically 25 minutes. You can use a physical timer, a timer app, or even a countdown feature on your phone.

Step 3: Work with Intense Focus

During the 25-minute Pomodoro interval, immerse yourself in your chosen task with undivided attention. Avoid any distractions, such as checking emails, social media, or unrelated tasks.

Step 4: Avoid Interruptions

Commit to maintaining your focus during the entire Pomodoro. If you encounter distractions or thoughts unrelated to the task, jot them down on a notepad and return to them during your break.

Step 5: Take a Short Break

When the timer goes off after 25 minutes, immediately stop working and take a 5-minute break. Use this time to relax, stretch, grab a snack, or simply clear your mind.

Step 6: Repeat the Process

After the short break, return to the task and set the timer for another 25-minute Pomodoro. Continue this cycle of focused work and short breaks until you've completed four Pomodoros.

Step 7: Take a Longer Break

After completing four Pomodoros (approximately 2 hours of focused work), reward yourself with a longer break of 15-30 minutes. Use this time to step away from your workspace, go for a walk, or engage in an activity you enjoy.

Step 8: Rinse and Repeat

Return to the cycle of Pomodoros and breaks as needed throughout your workday. Be consistent in maintaining the 25-minute work intervals and the regular breaks.

Benefits of the Process:

- **Enhanced Focus:** Breaking tasks into intervals ensures that you maintain high levels of focus and productivity during the work periods.

- **Reduced Procrastination:** The time-bound nature of Pomodoros minimizes the temptation to procrastinate since the work period is relatively short and manageable.

- **Increased Discipline:** The commitment to work during the Pomodoro intervals cultivates discipline and prevents distractions from derailing your efforts.

- **Regular Breaks:** The short breaks prevent burnout and mental fatigue, allowing you to recharge and return to tasks with renewed energy.

- **Motivation and Momentum:** Completing Pomodoros creates a sense of accomplishment, which boosts motivation and creates momentum throughout the day.

By adhering to this process of breaking tasks into focused intervals followed by short breaks, you'll discover a heightened ability to manage your time effectively, maintain concentration, and conquer laziness by transforming work into a series of achievable steps.

Tips for Implementing the Pomodoro Technique for Maximum Productivity:

1. Set Clear Goals:
Clearly define what you intend to accomplish during each Pomodoro session. Having a specific goal will help you stay focused and motivated throughout the interval.

2. Choose Appropriate Tasks:
Select tasks that can be completed within a 25-minute Pomodoro interval. Breaking larger tasks into smaller sub-tasks ensures a sense of accomplishment with each session.

3. Eliminate Distractions:
Create a distraction-free environment during your Pomodoro. Turn off notifications, close irrelevant tabs, and communicate to others that you're in a focused work mode.

4. Use a Timer:
Utilize a timer to track your Pomodoro intervals and breaks. Numerous Pomodoro timer apps are available that offer customizable settings to suit your preferences.

5. Take Breaks Seriously:
Use your 5-minute breaks to rest and recharge. Step away from your workspace, stretch, take deep breaths, or do a quick mindfulness exercise to clear your mind.

6. Adjust Interval Lengths:
While the traditional Pomodoro interval is 25 minutes, you can adjust the length based on your attention span and task requirements. Experiment to find the ideal duration for you.

7. Pomodoro Technique Variations:
Explore variations like the "90-20-90" technique, where you

work for 90 minutes, take a 20-minute break, and then continue with two more 90-minute work sessions.

8. Track Your Progress:
Keep a log of completed Pomodoros and the tasks you accomplished during each session. Tracking your progress helps you monitor your productivity and make improvements.

9. Batch Similar Tasks:
Group similar tasks together in a Pomodoro session. This reduces mental switching and allows you to maintain focus on a specific category of work.

10. Prioritize and Plan:
Before starting a Pomodoro, decide which task you'll work on. Prioritize tasks based on their importance and urgency, ensuring that your efforts align with your goals.

11. Utilize Longer Breaks:
During your longer breaks, engage in activities that truly relax and rejuvenate you. Stepping away from work entirely can boost your creativity and problem-solving abilities.

12. Tackle Procrastination Head-On:
If a task seems particularly daunting, commit to working on it for just one Pomodoro. Often, getting started is the biggest hurdle.

13. Practice Mindfulness:
During your Pomodoro intervals, practice mindfulness by focusing your attention solely on the task at hand. This practice enhances your concentration and reduces mental clutter.

14. Share Your Technique:
If you're working in a shared space, inform colleagues or family members about your Pomodoro sessions. This awareness can lead to a more supportive and respectful

environment.

15. Continuous Improvement:
Evaluate the effectiveness of the Pomodoro Technique for your productivity. Tweak your approach based on what works best for you, whether that's adjusting interval lengths or optimizing break activities.

Implementing the Pomodoro Technique requires dedication and consistency, but it's a powerful tool to enhance productivity and overcome the pull of laziness. By adhering to the structured intervals and breaks, you'll create a rhythm of focused work and rejuvenation that maximizes your output and fosters a deep sense of accomplishment.

Recommended Apps and Tools to Enhance Your Pomodoro Technique Experience:

1. Forest: Stay Focused, Be Present (Mobile App)
Forest combines the Pomodoro Technique with a gamified approach. Plant virtual trees during your work sessions, and if you stay focused, your tree grows. The app encourages you to avoid distractions and build a virtual forest of productivity.

2. Focus Booster (Web and Mobile App)
Focus Booster offers a simple and intuitive timer with customizable Pomodoro intervals and break durations. It also provides reports to track your work sessions and identify patterns in your productivity.

3. Pomodone (Web and Desktop App)
Pomodone integrates with various task management apps like Trello, Asana, and Todoist. It syncs your Pomodoro sessions with your task list, helping you stay organized and focused.

4. TomatoTimer (Web App)

TomatoTimer is a straightforward and free online timer designed specifically for the Pomodoro Technique. It offers preset Pomodoro intervals and breaks to get you started quickly.

5. Be Focused (Mobile App)

Be Focused offers a clean and user-friendly interface for implementing the Pomodoro Technique on your mobile device. It syncs with Apple devices, making it convenient for iOS users.

6. Focus@Will (Web and Mobile App)

Focus@Will provides background music designed to enhance concentration and focus. The app adapts its playlists based on your preferences and the task at hand.

7. Marinara Timer (Web App)

Marinara Timer offers customizable intervals for the Pomodoro Technique, as well as variations like the "52-17" technique. It's useful for experimenting with different time ratios.

8. PomoDoneApp (Web and Desktop App)

PomoDoneApp integrates with popular task management tools like Trello, Slack, and Google Calendar. It allows you to track your Pomodoro sessions and breaks directly within your existing workflows.

9. Focus Booster (Web and Mobile App)

Focus Booster provides a visually pleasing timer that tracks your Pomodoro sessions and breaks. It generates reports to help you analyze your productivity patterns over time.

10. Tomighty (Desktop App)

Tomighty is a lightweight desktop application that mimics a physical Pomodoro timer. It provides a minimalist way to implement the technique without distractions.

11. Engross: Focus Timer (Mobile App)

Engross offers a Pomodoro timer along with statistics and insights into your productivity habits. It's designed to help you develop better focus and time management skills.

Remember that the effectiveness of any app or tool depends on your personal preferences and workflow. Experiment with a few options to find the one that seamlessly integrates into your routine and helps you make the most of the Pomodoro Technique to combat laziness and boost your productivity.

CHAPTER 4: SHOSHIN - EMBRACING THE BEGINNER'S MIND

In a world saturated with routines and expectations, the concept of "shoshin" offers a refreshing approach to overcoming laziness and revitalizing productivity. Translating to "beginner's mind" in Japanese, shoshin encourages us to approach every task and experience with the curiosity and openness of a beginner. This mindset is free from preconceptions and biases, allowing us to view even the most familiar situations through fresh eyes.

Why Shoshin Matters:
In the context of combating laziness, shoshin is a powerful tool. Often, our familiarity with tasks can lead to complacency and a sense of monotony, fostering laziness in the process. Shoshin challenges us to break free from these patterns. By adopting the perspective of a beginner, we invite new perspectives and ideas, thereby rekindling our enthusiasm and motivation.

Breaking Down Barriers:
Shoshin dissolves the barriers created by fixed mindsets. When we approach tasks with a shoshin mindset, we're less likely to succumb to the paralysis of perfectionism or procrastination.

Shoshin encourages us to engage in tasks without the burden of past experiences, mistakes, or self-doubt, allowing us to tackle challenges with a fresh perspective.

Embracing the Unfamiliar:
Shoshin invites us to embrace the unfamiliar, the unexplored, and the uncertain. By shedding the limitations of what we think we know, we open ourselves up to growth and new learning opportunities. This adaptability is a cornerstone in the fight against laziness, as it enables us to navigate obstacles with resilience and creativity.

Cultivating Shoshin:
Cultivating a shoshin mindset requires conscious effort. It involves letting go of assumptions, biases, and the weight of past experiences. By embracing curiosity and humility, we empower ourselves to approach tasks as opportunities for growth. Shoshin encourages us to be open to failures and successes alike, ultimately nurturing a mindset that thrives on progress rather than perfection.

Overcoming Fixed Mindsets

In a world that often rewards expertise and mastery, fixed mindsets can inadvertently breed laziness and hinder progress. Fixed mindsets close the door to growth by limiting our willingness to try new things or approach tasks with an open mind. Shoshin, the beginner's mind, challenges these fixed mindsets by encouraging us to discard assumptions and embrace the unknown.

Shoshin's Role in Combating Fixed Mindsets:
Shoshin breathes new life into our approach to tasks. It dismantles the notion that we've learned all we need to know about a particular topic or task. Instead of allowing laziness to stem from the belief that we have nothing new to gain, shoshin pushes us to approach every endeavor as an opportunity to learn,

grow, and evolve.

The Power of Unlearning:
Fixed mindsets often prevent us from unlearning outdated or counterproductive habits. Shoshin invites us to unburden ourselves from these mental shackles. By stripping away outdated assumptions, we make space for innovative ideas and renewed enthusiasm.

Embracing Curiosity and Growth

One of the key aspects of the shoshin mindset is its emphasis on curiosity and growth. While familiarity can lead to complacency, shoshin encourages us to view every task as a chance to explore, learn, and develop new skills. This approach directly counteracts laziness by igniting our passion for improvement.

Shoshin's Impact on Curiosity:
Shoshin breathes life into our innate curiosity. When we approach tasks with the fresh perspective of a beginner, we naturally ask questions and seek to understand deeply. This curiosity propels us forward and fuels our motivation to overcome laziness.

Renewed Appreciation for the Present Moment:
Shoshin invites us to see the present moment with new eyes. Instead of allowing laziness to stem from routine, shoshin encourages us to engage fully in the now. This presence fosters a sense of mindfulness and heightened awareness, enhancing our ability to stay focused and productive.

The Path to Growth:
By embracing the growth-oriented mindset of shoshin, we pave the way for continuous self-improvement. Rather than resting on our laurels, we see every task as an opportunity to advance, fostering a sense of accomplishment that becomes a driving force against the inertia of laziness.

Shoshin in Practice

Cultivating a beginner's mindset, or shoshin, is a transformative journey that requires conscious effort and practice. Here, we'll explore actionable tips and techniques to help you infuse the essence of shoshin into your daily life, enabling you to overcome laziness and embrace the power of fresh perspectives.

1. Approach Tasks with Curiosity:
View each task as an opportunity to learn something new. Ask questions, explore different angles, and seek to understand deeply. This shift in perspective can invigorate your approach and reignite your motivation.

2. Release Assumptions:
Recognize that your past experiences might not always apply to new situations. Challenge the assumptions that arise and be open to alternative viewpoints. This practice breaks the cycle of laziness by allowing you to engage with tasks without preconceived notions.

3. Embrace Mistakes:
A beginner's mindset welcomes mistakes as valuable learning experiences. Rather than fearing failure, see it as a chance to gather insights and improve. This mindset shift reduces the fear of making mistakes that can sometimes contribute to procrastination.

4. Stay Present:
Focusing on the present moment prevents your mind from wandering to past mistakes or future uncertainties. By practicing mindfulness, you can fully engage with tasks, minimizing the pull of laziness and boosting your productivity.

5. Explore Unfamiliar Territory:
Challenge yourself to step outside your comfort zone and explore new areas. This can range from trying a different approach to a

familiar task or delving into a completely new skill. Embracing the unfamiliar keeps your mind engaged and prevents monotony-induced laziness.

6. Let Go of Labels:
Labels and titles can limit your potential. Instead of defining yourself by what you know, approach tasks with a willingness to learn and adapt. This outlook breaks down mental barriers that contribute to fixed mindsets and laziness.

7. Cultivate a Learning Mindset:
Foster the belief that you are in a constant state of growth and learning. Seek out opportunities to acquire new knowledge, whether through books, courses, or conversations. This mindset fuels your motivation to overcome inertia.

By integrating these actionable tips into your daily routine, you'll gradually embrace the transformative power of shoshin. As you release preconceived notions and welcome new perspectives, you'll find yourself overcoming the obstacles of laziness and rediscovering the excitement of continuous growth and productivity.

Shoshin vs. Procrastination

Shoshin, the beginner's mind, serves as a powerful antidote to the insidious tendencies of procrastination. By its very nature, shoshin challenges the root causes of procrastination and paves the way for renewed motivation and productivity. Let's delve into how shoshin counters procrastination and explore examples of how it breaks through the inertia of laziness.

Shoshin's Role in Overcoming Procrastination:
1. **Fresh Perspective:** Procrastination often emerges from a sense of monotony and disinterest. Shoshin infuses tasks with newness, reigniting your curiosity and reducing the inclination to delay.

2. **Reduced Perfectionism:** Shoshin encourages you to let go of perfectionism. When you approach tasks with the humility of a beginner, you're more likely to start without getting trapped in the cycle of overthinking.

3. **Mindfulness in Action:** Shoshin promotes mindfulness by keeping you grounded in the present moment. Procrastination thrives on distractions and avoidance; shoshin's focus on the now combats these tendencies.

Examples of Shoshin Breaking Inertia:

1. **Learning a New Skill:** Imagine tackling a skill you've always wanted to learn, like playing an instrument. Shoshin encourages you to start with excitement, allowing you to bypass the resistance that might arise from thinking it's too late or too difficult.

2. **Beginning a Project:** Shoshin can propel you to initiate a project you've been putting off. By approaching it with the openness of a beginner, you dismantle the barriers that contribute to procrastination.

3. **Facing Mundane Tasks:** Even routine tasks benefit from shoshin. When doing chores or administrative work, a beginner's mindset introduces an element of curiosity and engagement, making the task more enticing.

4. **Overcoming Writer's Block:** Writers often struggle with procrastination. Shoshin helps by inviting you to write without judgment, allowing creativity to flow more freely.

5. **Breaking Study Procrastination:** When faced with studying, shoshin encourages you to approach the material as though it's entirely new. This shift can invigorate your engagement and lead to improved retention.

Shoshin's ability to counteract procrastination is rooted in its emphasis on curiosity, presence, and growth. By applying the principles of the beginner's mind, you can break through the barriers of laziness and embark on tasks with a renewed sense of purpose and enthusiasm.

Exercises for Cultivating Shoshin

Cultivating the essence of shoshin, the beginner's mind, involves deliberate practice and reflection. The following exercises are designed to nurture this mindset, helping you break free from the grip of laziness and unlock the transformative power of fresh perspectives. Engage in these exercises to infuse shoshin into your daily routine and promote ongoing self-growth.

1. Task Reimagining:
Choose a familiar task you often approach with a sense of laziness or monotony. Imagine you're encountering it for the first time. How would you approach it? What questions would you ask? Apply this new perspective to the task, and notice how it changes your experience.

2. Mindful Exploration:
Engage in an activity you typically rush through, such as eating a meal or taking a walk. Pay attention to the details you usually overlook. Reflect on the sensations, colors, sounds, and scents you encounter. This exercise fosters mindfulness and encourages you to engage fully in the present moment.

3. Unlearning Assumptions:
Choose a topic or skill you're knowledgeable about. List the assumptions you hold. Now, challenge each assumption and explore alternative viewpoints. This exercise encourages you to shed preconceived notions and approach the subject with the openness of a beginner.

4. Future Self-Reflection:
Visualize yourself a year from now, having cultivated the shoshin mindset consistently. How have your productivity and

mindset transformed? What opportunities have you embraced? Write a letter to your future self, outlining the growth and accomplishments you envision.

5. Task Innovation:
Select a task you've been postponing due to laziness. Brainstorm alternative ways to approach it, as if you were tackling it for the first time. List three innovative approaches, and commit to trying one of them. This exercise injects novelty into your approach and helps combat procrastination.

6. Curiosity Journaling:
Set aside a few minutes each day to jot down questions that spark your curiosity. These questions can pertain to any aspect of your life. Use this exercise to fuel your desire to learn and explore, fostering a shoshin mindset.

7. Reflective Evaluation:
At the end of each day, reflect on your activities. Identify moments when you embraced shoshin and moments when laziness crept in. Consider what factors influenced each mindset. Use this reflection to refine your practice and reinforce shoshin-oriented behaviors.

By engaging in these exercises, you'll actively foster the shoshin mindset, paving the way for personal growth, enhanced productivity, and a heightened ability to overcome laziness. Embrace the beginner's mind and embark on a journey of continuous learning and transformation.

Real-Life Shoshin Stories

Real-life stories of individuals who have embraced the shoshin mindset exemplify the transformative power of approaching life with a beginner's mind. These stories showcase how shoshin has broken through the inertia of laziness, leading to remarkable accomplishments and personal growth.

Story 1: Rediscovering Passion

Marina, a marketing executive, found herself in a slump, struggling to find motivation in her routine tasks. Inspired by shoshin, she rekindled her curiosity and approached each project as an opportunity to learn. Her newfound enthusiasm led to innovative campaigns and breakthrough ideas, ultimately reviving her passion for her work and transforming her productivity.

Story 2: Overcoming Creative Block

Michael, an artist, faced a prolonged creative block that left him feeling uninspired and unproductive. Embracing the shoshin mindset, he began to approach his art with the openness of a beginner. By letting go of self-imposed expectations, he experimented with new techniques and mediums. This exploration not only revitalized his creativity but also led to a series of successful exhibitions and collaborations.

Story 3: Professional Growth

Lena had been avoiding public speaking due to a fear of failure. Shoshin gave her the courage to approach public speaking with curiosity rather than trepidation. She enrolled in workshops, studied renowned speakers, and gradually refined her skills. Her commitment to learning and growth allowed her to overcome her fear, and she now speaks confidently at conferences, inspiring others with her journey.

Story 4: Entrepreneurial Success

Jacob, an aspiring entrepreneur, was hesitant to start his own business due to the fear of failure. Shoshin transformed his perspective, encouraging him to embrace each step of the entrepreneurial journey as a learning experience. With this mindset, he launched his business, accepting challenges and setbacks as opportunities to refine his approach. His dedication paid off, and his business grew exponentially, defying the grasp of laziness and doubt.

Story 5: Personal Renewal

Emily had been feeling stuck in her personal life, struggling to break free from a routine that left her feeling unfulfilled. Through shoshin, she began to approach everyday activities with fresh eyes. This mindset of openness led her to new hobbies, friendships, and experiences she had never considered before. Shoshin revitalized her sense of purpose and instilled a sense of adventure, inspiring her to pursue her dreams with renewed vigor.

These real-life stories illustrate how shoshin, the beginner's mind, has the capacity to invigorate lives and fuel remarkable accomplishments. By embracing curiosity, openness, and growth, individuals have overcome the inertia of laziness and transformed their paths in profound ways. These stories stand as a testament to the enduring power of shoshin to reshape lives and unlock hidden potential.

CHAPTER 5: GAMAN - HARNESSING PERSEVERANCE AND ENDURANCE FOR SUCCESS

In the realm of overcoming challenges, the Japanese concept of "Gaman" stands as a powerful embodiment of resilience and unwavering determination. Rooted in the cultural ethos of perseverance, Gaman is a principle that teaches us to endure difficulties and setbacks with grace and strength. This chapter delves into the essence of Gaman, exploring its origins, cultural significance, and how it serves as a guiding light to overcome obstacles and combat the insidious grasp of laziness.

Understanding Gaman:

Derived from the Japanese word for "endure" or "tolerate," Gaman embodies the idea of accepting hardships and adversities without complaint or resistance. It goes beyond mere endurance, emphasizing a noble and dignified approach to facing challenges.

Gaman teaches us to cultivate patience, inner strength, and a steadfast spirit, even in the face of difficulties that may tempt us to give in to laziness.

Cultural Significance:

Gaman is deeply ingrained in Japanese culture and history. It emerged as a coping mechanism during times of hardship, such as wars and natural disasters. It's a reflection of the collective resilience of the Japanese people, who have historically exhibited the strength to persevere through adversity. This cultural value is evident in everyday life, from the stoic determination of artisans perfecting their craft to the patience displayed in traditional tea ceremonies.

Gaman's Connection to Overcoming Laziness:

The concept of Gaman holds valuable lessons for combating laziness:

1. **Inner Resilience:** Gaman teaches us to develop inner resilience that enables us to weather challenges and setbacks without succumbing to laziness or despair.

2. **Long-Term Focus:** Gaman encourages a focus on long-term goals, reminding us that momentary discomfort or difficulties should not deter us from our overarching objectives.

3. **Endurance Through Patience:** By embracing Gaman, we learn to tolerate temporary discomfort and work steadily towards our goals, even when faced with obstacles that might otherwise lead to laziness.

4. **Dignified Effort:** Gaman emphasizes dignified effort and commitment. This mindset cultivates a sense of pride in overcoming adversity, making the temptation of laziness less appealing.

Applying Gaman in Daily Life:

1. **Embrace Challenges:** Approach challenges with an open heart and the willingness to learn and grow. Embracing difficulty as an opportunity can help combat laziness.

2. **Set Long-Term Goals:** Define clear and meaningful long-term goals that provide a sense of purpose and direction, motivating you to persist even in the face of laziness.

3. **Focus on Process:** Instead of fixating on immediate results, focus on the journey and the progress you make. This perspective promotes consistency and discourages laziness.

4. **Cultivate Patience:** Develop the patience to work through challenges step by step. This patience diminishes the appeal of taking shortcuts or giving in to laziness.

5. **Practice Mindfulness:** Cultivate mindfulness to stay present and fully engage in your efforts, reducing the likelihood of getting sidetracked by laziness.

In Conclusion:

Gaman is a principle that empowers us to endure, persist, and triumph over the allure of laziness. By embracing challenges with resilience and determination, we navigate through obstacles and setbacks while maintaining our focus on meaningful objectives. Through Gaman, we elevate our efforts to a level of honorable commitment, transcending momentary difficulties and paving the way for enduring success. This chapter guides you through the essence of Gaman and its practical application, equipping you with the wisdom to harness perseverance and endurance to conquer laziness and achieve your goals.

Cultivating Perseverance to Overcome Feelings of Laziness:

Developing a mindset of perseverance is a powerful tool to counteract feelings of laziness. It equips you with the mental strength and determination to push through obstacles, maintain focus on your goals, and resist the pull of inertia. Here's how cultivating perseverance can help you overcome laziness:

1. Clarifies Your Purpose:
A clear sense of purpose drives perseverance. When you have a strong "why" behind your actions, you're more likely to stay committed and motivated, even when laziness creeps in.

2. Focuses on Long-Term Goals:
Perseverance directs your attention to long-term goals rather than immediate gratification. This shift in focus helps you resist the short-term allure of laziness and keeps you on track toward your aspirations.

3. Builds Mental Resilience:
A persistent mindset strengthens your mental resilience. You learn to cope with challenges, setbacks, and failures without losing motivation or succumbing to laziness.

4. Embraces Discomfort:
Perseverance involves embracing discomfort and pushing through difficult moments. By doing so, you develop a tolerance for discomfort, making laziness less appealing.

5. Promotes Consistency:
Perseverance encourages consistency in your efforts. Consistency erodes the habit of laziness and replaces it with a habit of determined action.

6. Overcomes Procrastination:
Procrastination often stems from feelings of laziness. Perseverance combats procrastination by helping you start tasks and sustain your efforts, even when motivation wanes.

7. Fosters a Growth Mindset:

A mindset of perseverance is closely tied to a growth mindset. You view challenges as opportunities for growth, which reduces the likelihood of succumbing to laziness when faced with difficulty.

8. Creates a Sense of Accomplishment:
Overcoming challenges and staying committed to your goals generate a sense of accomplishment. This feeling of achievement acts as a counterbalance to laziness.

9. Eliminates Regret:
Perseverance prevents the regret that often accompanies giving in to laziness. You know that you've done your best and pursued your goals wholeheartedly.

10. Increases Self-Discipline:
Developing perseverance requires self-discipline. As your self-discipline improves, you gain better control over your impulses and become less susceptible to laziness.

Practical Steps to Cultivate Perseverance:

1. **Set Clear Goals:** Clearly define your goals to give yourself a sense of purpose and direction.

2. **Break Tasks Down:** Divide larger goals into smaller, manageable tasks. Each completion builds your sense of accomplishment and fights laziness.

3. **Create a Routine:** Establish a consistent routine that includes dedicated time for tasks. Routine minimizes the impact of laziness by making tasks habitual.

4. **Visualize Success:** Imagine the positive outcomes of your efforts. Visualization can motivate you to persist and overcome feelings of laziness.

5. **Reward Progress:** Reward yourself for completing tasks or reaching milestones. Positive reinforcement reinforces your commitment and weakens laziness.

6. **Embrace Challenges:** Welcome challenges as opportunities for growth. A persistent mindset frames challenges as stepping stones, making laziness less tempting.

7. **Practice Patience:** Cultivate patience as you work toward your goals. Recognize that progress takes time, and perseverance is key to success.

By adopting a mindset of perseverance, you empower yourself to tackle laziness head-on. Through consistent effort, determination, and a focus on your long-term objectives, you'll build resilience against the pull of inertia and cultivate a productive, fulfilled life.

Stories of Resilience and Gaman:

1. Hiroki Nakauchi - Rebuilding After the Tsunami:

After the devastating 2011 tsunami in Japan, Hiroki Nakauchi's family lost their fishery business. Despite the immense loss, Nakauchi displayed Gaman by embracing his role as a torchbearer for his family's legacy. He rebuilt the business from scratch, demonstrating unwavering determination and perseverance.

2. Jiro Ono - Pursuit of Culinary Excellence:

Jiro Ono, the renowned sushi master, exemplified Gaman throughout his culinary journey. For decades, he tirelessly honed his craft, facing challenges and setbacks while striving for perfection. His dedication to mastering the art of sushi-making showcases the resilience and patience inherent in Gaman.

3. Chiune Sugihara - The "Japanese Schindler":

Chiune Sugihara, a Japanese diplomat during World War II, defied orders to save thousands of Jewish refugees by issuing transit visas. Sugihara's courageous act required immense perseverance and inner strength, as he risked his career and personal safety to do what he believed was right.

4. Naomi Osaka - Rising Above Adversity:

Tennis star Naomi Osaka faced numerous challenges on her path to success. She encountered racism, skepticism, and self-doubt. Yet, Osaka's Gaman was evident as she persisted, eventually becoming a Grand Slam champion and a role model for young athletes.

5. Sadako Sasaki - Folding a Thousand Cranes:

Sadako Sasaki, a victim of the Hiroshima atomic bombing, developed leukemia at a young age. Inspired by the Japanese tradition that folding a thousand paper cranes grants a wish, Sadako folded cranes with unwavering determination despite her declining health. Her story of Gaman and hope continues to inspire people worldwide.

6. Masazo Nonaka - World's Oldest Man:

Masazo Nonaka, recognized as the world's oldest man, displayed Gaman throughout his life. Living to over 112 years old, Nonaka faced the challenges of time with grace and determination, embracing each day and preserving his positive spirit.

7. Seiko Hashimoto - Olympian and Leader:

Seiko Hashimoto, a former Olympic athlete and now a leader in Japanese sports administration, showcased Gaman by transitioning from a successful athletic career to contributing to the sports community. Her tenacity and ability to navigate various challenges demonstrate the enduring spirit of Gaman.

8. Isamu Akasaki, Hiroshi Amano, and Shuji Nakamura - LED Innovators:

These three scientists worked persistently on developing blue LED technology, a breakthrough that earned them the Nobel Prize in Physics. Despite facing technical obstacles and skepticism, their dedication to their vision exemplifies

Gaman's essence.

9. Tamae Watanabe - Conquering Mount Everest:

Tamae Watanabe, a Japanese mountaineer, became the oldest woman to summit Mount Everest at the age of 73. Her achievement was the result of years of dedication, training, and unwavering determination. Watanabe's Gaman was evident in her perseverance through grueling conditions and her commitment to achieving a feat that required physical and mental endurance.

10. Kazuo Inamori - Entrepreneur and Philanthropist:

Kazuo Inamori, the founder of Kyocera and KDDI Corporation, exemplified Gaman throughout his career. He turned around struggling companies and transformed them into successful enterprises through sheer determination, hard work, and a relentless pursuit of excellence. Inamori's commitment to his vision and his ability to face challenges with unwavering resolve showcase the power of Gaman in achieving extraordinary results. Later in life, he also founded the Inamori Foundation and the Kyoto Prize, demonstrating his commitment to giving back to society and inspiring future generations.

These stories of individuals from different walks of life showcase the power of Gaman in overcoming challenges, pursuing excellence, and persevering despite adversity. Their journeys inspire us to develop our own resilience, demonstrating that a mindset of determination and perseverance can lead to remarkable accomplishments, even in the face of laziness or obstacles.

Practical Techniques to Strengthen Endurance and Persistence:

1. Set Clear Goals:

Clearly define your short-term and long-term goals. Knowing what you're working toward gives you a sense of purpose and direction, making it easier to endure challenges.

2. Break Tasks into Smaller Steps:
Divide larger tasks into smaller, manageable steps. Achieving these smaller milestones provides a sense of accomplishment and keeps you motivated.

3. Visualize Success:
Imagine yourself successfully overcoming challenges and achieving your goals. Visualization can boost your confidence and motivation to persist.

4. Practice Self-Compassion:
Treat yourself with kindness and understanding, especially when facing setbacks. Self-compassion encourages you to keep going despite difficulties.

5. Stay Mindful:
Practice mindfulness to stay present and centered. Mindfulness helps you navigate challenges with clarity and reduce feelings of overwhelm.

6. Celebrate Progress:
Acknowledge and celebrate even small successes along the way. Recognizing your progress boosts your motivation and determination.

7. Develop a Routine:
Establish a daily routine that includes dedicated time for tasks related to your goals. Routine creates consistency and minimizes decision fatigue.

8. Seek Support:
Surround yourself with a supportive network of friends, family, or mentors who can offer encouragement and guidance during challenging times.

9. Learn from Setbacks:
View setbacks as opportunities for growth and learning. Analyze what went wrong and use the insights to improve your approach.

10. Embrace Failure as Feedback:
Shift your perspective on failure. See it as feedback that helps you refine your strategies and become more resilient.

11. Practice Perseverance Daily:
Cultivate the habit of persistence in everyday tasks. When you consistently overcome small challenges, you build your endurance muscle.

12. Focus on Process, Not Just Results:
Place importance on the effort you put into tasks, not just the immediate outcomes. A focus on process reinforces your commitment to endurance.

13. Maintain a Positive Mindset:
Cultivate a positive attitude by focusing on the potential benefits of persistence and the opportunities that challenge present.

14. Develop a Growth Mindset:
Embrace challenges as opportunities for growth. A growth mindset helps you see setbacks as temporary and solvable.

15. Practice Delayed Gratification:
Train yourself to prioritize long-term rewards over short-term comfort or pleasure. This helps you endure challenges for greater gains.

16. Reflect on Past Successes:
Recall times when you persevered and succeeded. Remind yourself of your inner strength and capacity for endurance.

17. Stay Committed Through Discomfort:
Recognize that discomfort is often a part of growth. Commit

to persisting even when things feel difficult or uncertain.

18. Journal Your Journey:
Keep a journal to document your progress, challenges, and feelings. Reflecting on your journey can provide valuable insights and motivation.

19. Practice Resilience-Building Activities:
Engage in activities like meditation, exercise, or creative outlets that boost your mental and emotional resilience.

20. Keep Learning and Adapting:
Stay open to learning new skills and adjusting your strategies. Adaptability is a key trait in enduring challenges.

By incorporating these practical techniques into your daily life, you can strengthen your ability to endure challenges, persist through difficulties, and ultimately overcome feelings of laziness or discouragement. Remember that building endurance is a gradual process, and each step you take contributes to your personal growth and success.

CHAPTER 6: KAIZEN MINDSET - EMBRACING CHANGE FOR CONTINUOUS IMPROVEMENT

In the pursuit of personal growth and overcoming laziness, the Kaizen philosophy offers a transformative approach rooted in the concept of continuous improvement. Originating from Japan, Kaizen emphasizes making small, incremental changes to achieve lasting progress. This chapter delves deeper into the Kaizen philosophy, its profound impact on mindset, and how adopting a Kaizen mindset can empower you to conquer laziness and thrive in your endeavors.

Understanding Kaizen:

Kaizen, derived from the Japanese words "kai" (change) and "zen" (good), advocates the philosophy of making gradual, positive changes over time. It acknowledges that significant transformations often stem from consistent, small adjustments that accumulate to produce remarkable results. This philosophy permeates various aspects of Japanese culture, from manufacturing to personal development.

Embracing Change Through Kaizen:

The Kaizen mindset encourages you to embrace change as an opportunity for growth. It shifts your perspective from perceiving change as daunting to seeing it as a natural part of improvement. This mindset empowers you to:

1. **Overcome Resistance:** Kaizen helps you overcome resistance to change by breaking it down into manageable steps, reducing the fear and inertia associated with tackling significant changes.

2. **Counteract Laziness:** By focusing on small, achievable goals, the Kaizen approach minimizes the overwhelming feeling that can lead to laziness. Each step feels attainable and motivating.

3. **Cultivate a Learning Attitude:** The Kaizen philosophy promotes a learning attitude, emphasizing that every step, regardless of its size, offers an opportunity to learn and grow.

4. **Enhance Self-Discipline:** Kaizen reinforces self-discipline as you commit to making consistent, incremental improvements. This discipline helps counteract the allure of laziness.

5. **Increase Adaptability:** A Kaizen mindset fosters adaptability, enabling you to respond positively to change and new challenges rather than resisting or feeling overwhelmed.

6. **Build Confidence:** Each small success in the Kaizen journey builds your confidence, making it easier to take on more significant challenges without succumbing to laziness.

Applying Kaizen to Overcome Laziness:

1. **Set Micro-Goals:** Break larger goals into smaller, achievable micro-goals. These bite-sized tasks are less likely to trigger feelings of laziness.

2. **Focus on the Present:** Kaizen encourages you to focus on the present and the incremental changes you can make today, eliminating the overwhelm that leads to laziness.

3. **Embrace Imperfection:** The Kaizen philosophy acknowledges that progress is imperfect but continuous. This mindset combats the perfectionism that can contribute to laziness.

4. **Celebrate Small Wins:** Acknowledge and celebrate each small success. The act of celebrating helps motivate you and combats the demotivation of laziness.

5. **Seek Feedback:** Embrace feedback and use it to refine your approach. The Kaizen mindset values feedback as a tool for growth, preventing stagnation and laziness.

6. **Cultivate Patience:** Kaizen teaches patience as you commit to long-term growth. This patience counters the impatience that can lead to laziness.

In Conclusion:

The Kaizen philosophy inspires you to embrace change as an ally on your journey to overcome laziness and achieve continuous improvement. By adopting a Kaizen mindset, you shift your focus from daunting transformations to small, manageable steps that accumulate over time. Through the power of incremental change, you can conquer the inertia of laziness, fostering a sense of accomplishment and personal growth that empowers you to thrive. This chapter guides you through the essence of the Kaizen mindset, providing practical strategies to integrate it into your life and overcome the challenges of laziness.

The Importance of Embracing Change to Avoid Stagnation and

Complacency:

Change is an inevitable and essential aspect of life. Embracing change is not only about adapting to external circumstances but also about fostering personal growth, preventing stagnation, and avoiding the trap of complacency. Here's why embracing change is crucial for your overall well-being and success:

1. Cultivates Personal Growth:

Change challenges you to step out of your comfort zone, learn new skills, and expand your horizons. Embracing change fosters continuous personal growth, allowing you to evolve as an individual and avoid remaining stagnant.

2. Promotes Adaptability:

Life is dynamic, and situations are subject to change. Embracing change enhances your adaptability, enabling you to navigate challenges with resilience and creativity.

3. Prevents Stagnation:

Stagnation occurs when you remain in the same routine, refusing to explore new possibilities. Embracing change injects freshness into your life, preventing boredom and the sense of being stuck.

4. Encourages Innovation:

Change sparks innovation and creativity. When you're open to new ideas and ways of doing things, you're more likely to discover innovative solutions and opportunities.

5. Combats Complacency:

Complacency is the enemy of progress. Embracing change prevents you from settling for mediocrity and encourages you to continually challenge yourself.

6. Boosts Resilience:

Change often comes with challenges, but navigating those challenges builds resilience. Embracing change equips you with the skills to bounce back from setbacks.

7. Enhances Learning:
Change presents opportunities to learn and adapt. Whether it's acquiring new knowledge or refining your skills, each change serves as a learning experience.

8. Expands Perspective:
Embracing change exposes you to diverse viewpoints and experiences. This expanded perspective enriches your understanding of the world and contributes to personal development.

9. Increases Confidence:
Successfully navigating changes and overcoming challenges boosts your confidence. This newfound self-assurance encourages you to take on more significant challenges and resist complacency.

10. Fuels Personal Satisfaction:
Progress and growth contribute to a sense of personal satisfaction and fulfillment. Embracing change ensures that you're consistently moving forward on your journey.

11. Encourages Risk-Taking:
Change often involves taking calculated risks. Embracing change encourages you to step out of your comfort zone and embrace uncertainty, which can lead to greater rewards.

12. Keeps Goals Relevant:
As your circumstances change, so do your goals and priorities. Embracing change helps you align your goals with your current situation, preventing them from becoming outdated or irrelevant.

13. Prevents Regret:
Avoiding change can lead to regret later in life. Regret often stems from missed opportunities that could have contributed to personal growth and fulfillment.

14. Fosters a Growth Mindset:
Embracing change is a key component of a growth mindset. It reinforces the belief that challenges are opportunities for growth rather than obstacles to avoid.

In essence, embracing change is an active choice that empowers you to lead a dynamic, fulfilling life. It's a countermeasure against stagnation and complacency that can lead to feelings of laziness. By adopting a mindset that embraces change as an ally, you position yourself for continuous growth, enhanced adaptability, and a life rich with diverse experiences.

Steps for Adopting a Kaizen Mindset to Overcome the Inertia of Laziness:

1. Recognize the Power of Small Steps:
Acknowledge that significant progress can be achieved through consistent, small changes. Understand that taking small actions is more manageable and less overwhelming than attempting major transformations.

2. Set Micro-Goals:
Break your larger goals into tiny, achievable micro-goals. These small steps are less likely to trigger feelings of laziness and make progress feel attainable.

3. Start with the 1-Minute Rule:
Commit to working on a task for just one minute. Often, the most challenging part is getting started. Once you've begun, you're more likely to continue beyond that initial minute.

4. Prioritize Consistency:
Focus on making incremental changes consistently, rather than aiming for perfection or quick fixes. Consistency builds momentum and counters the inertia of laziness.

5. Create a Kaizen Plan:

Develop a plan that outlines the small changes you'll make over time. List the steps you'll take each day or week to work toward your goals.

6. Celebrate Small Wins:
Acknowledge and celebrate each small success. Celebrations provide positive reinforcement, motivating you to continue and diminishing the demotivation of laziness.

7. Practice Self-Compassion:
Be kind to yourself when setbacks occur. Embrace a mindset of self-compassion that encourages you to continue despite challenges or moments of laziness.

8. Focus on the Present Moment:
Concentrate on the small actions you can take today. Embrace each present moment as an opportunity for growth, rather than dwelling on past laziness.

9. Adapt and Iterate:
As you progress, evaluate the effectiveness of your small changes. Adjust your approach based on what's working and what isn't, in the spirit of continuous improvement.

10. Embrace Flexibility:
Be open to adjusting your goals and plans as needed. Flexibility prevents rigidity and frustration, which can contribute to feelings of laziness.

11. Practice Gratitude:
Cultivate gratitude for the progress you make, no matter how small. Gratitude fuels motivation and combats the negativity of laziness.

12. Challenge Perfectionism:
Release the need for perfection. Understand that incremental changes don't need to be flawless. Progress is more important than perfection.

13. Visualize Success:
Envision the positive outcomes of your small actions. Visualization enhances motivation and reduces the tendency to give in to laziness.

14. Seek Feedback and Adapt:
Welcome feedback from others or self-assessment. Use feedback to adjust your approach and make continuous improvements.

15. Create a Supportive Environment:
Surround yourself with people, resources, and environments that encourage your efforts toward continuous improvement and combat the pull of laziness.

16. Practice Patience:
Understand that change takes time. Cultivate patience and remind yourself that each small step contributes to your long-term goals.

By integrating these steps into your daily life, you can adopt a Kaizen mindset that gradually diminishes the inertia of laziness. Embracing the philosophy of continuous improvement empowers you to make consistent progress, even in the face of challenges. Over time, the accumulation of small actions will lead to substantial growth and achievement.

Exercises to Foster Adaptability and Openness to Growth:

1. Embrace Change Journaling:
Keep a journal to record moments when you embraced change willingly or instances where you resisted it. Reflect on how each situation impacted your growth and well-being.

2. Step Out of Your Comfort Zone:
Regularly engage in activities or experiences that are outside

your comfort zone. Start with small steps and gradually increase the complexity of challenges.

3. Try Something New Weekly:
Commit to trying something new each week, whether it's a new recipe, hobby, or social activity. Embrace the unfamiliar and practice adapting to change.

4. Mindful Exploration:
Engage in mindfulness exercises that focus on observing your thoughts and reactions to change. This practice increases self-awareness and reduces resistance.

5. Visualize Flexible Responses:
Practice visualization where you imagine yourself responding positively and adaptively to unexpected changes. This exercise trains your mind to be open to growth.

6. Reflect on Past Adaptations:
Recall instances in your life when you successfully adapted to change. Reflect on how those experiences enriched your life and contributed to your growth.

7. Seek Feedback Intentionally:
Ask friends, family, or colleagues for constructive feedback. Approach feedback as an opportunity for growth rather than criticism.

8. Limit Routine:
Purposefully disrupt your routine by introducing new elements. This exercise challenges your ability to adapt and reduces reliance on set patterns.

9. Reverse Negative Thinking:
When faced with change, consciously replace negative thoughts with positive or neutral ones. This practice rewires your mindset to view change as potential growth.

10. Open-Minded Conversations:

Engage in discussions with people who hold differing viewpoints. Practice listening actively and without judgment, fostering adaptability.

11. Role Reversal Exercise:
Put yourself in someone else's shoes and imagine how they perceive change. This empathy exercise enhances your ability to understand diverse perspectives.

12. Challenge Yourself Weekly:
Set a weekly challenge that requires you to adapt, whether it's learning a new skill, adjusting your routine, or navigating a different route to work.

13. Change Environment:
Rearrange your living or working space periodically. This physical change encourages mental flexibility and helps you become comfortable with adapting.

14. Elicit Change Plans:
Ask friends or family to introduce changes to your plans, forcing you to adapt and recalibrate. This exercise reduces rigidity and encourages adaptability.

15. Mindful Breathing Through Change:
Practice mindful breathing techniques when faced with unexpected changes. This exercise helps you manage stress and respond thoughtfully.

16. Growth Mindset Affirmations:
Develop a list of growth mindset affirmations that you can recite daily. These affirmations reinforce your openness to change and personal growth.

By incorporating these exercises into your routine, you can gradually enhance your adaptability and cultivate an open mindset towards growth. Embracing change becomes a natural part of your journey, helping you overcome resistance, reduce the impact of laziness, and foster a resilient approach to life's

BILL GALVESTON

challenges.

CHAPTER 7: WABI-SABI - EMBRACING IMPERFECTION FOR SELF-ACCEPTANCE AND AUTHENTICITY

In a world that often celebrates perfection and flawlessness, the Japanese concept of Wabi-Sabi stands as a beautiful reminder of the inherent beauty in imperfection and transience. Rooted in Zen philosophy and aesthetics, Wabi-Sabi encourages us to find solace and authenticity in the imperfect, the incomplete, and the impermanent. This chapter delves into the essence of Wabi-Sabi, its profound connection to self-acceptance, and how adopting its principles can help overcome feelings of laziness and foster a sense of genuine purpose.

Understanding Wabi-Sabi:

Wabi-Sabi is a Japanese term derived from "wabi" (the beauty of simplicity) and "sabi" (the beauty that comes with age and wear). This philosophy celebrates the beauty of imperfection, impermanence, and the authenticity of natural processes. It finds expression in art, architecture, and even the rhythm of daily life.

Embracing Imperfection and Authenticity:

Wabi-Sabi challenges the notion that perfection equates to beauty and value. Instead, it emphasizes the uniqueness and character found in flaws, weathering, and the passage of time. By embracing imperfection and authenticity, you can:

1. **Cultivate Self-Acceptance:** Wabi-Sabi encourages you to accept your own imperfections, quirks, and mistakes. This self-acceptance diminishes feelings of inadequacy that can lead to laziness.

2. **Reduce Perfectionism:** The pursuit of perfection can be paralyzing. Wabi-Sabi invites you to let go of rigid standards and appreciate the beauty in things as they are.

3. **Embrace the Present Moment:** Impermanence is a core aspect of Wabi-Sabi. By embracing the present moment and finding beauty in its fleeting nature, you cultivate mindfulness and counteract laziness.

4. **Appreciate the Journey:** Wabi-Sabi reminds us that the journey is as valuable as the destination. This perspective encourages you to engage fully in your efforts, reducing the temptation of laziness.

5. **Foster Genuine Connections:** Embracing authenticity allows you to connect more deeply with yourself and others. Authenticity combats the isolation that can result from feelings of laziness.

6. **Celebrate Uniqueness:** Just as a weathered object gains character, your unique qualities make you special. Embracing your individuality prevents the sense of homogeneity that can lead to laziness.

Applying Wabi-Sabi to Overcome Laziness:

1. **Reframe Perfectionism:** When striving for perfection, remind yourself of the beauty in imperfection. This shift reduces the pressure that contributes to laziness.

2. **Practice Self-Compassion:** Embrace self-compassion when you make mistakes or face setbacks. Self-compassion discourages the self-criticism that fuels laziness.

3. **Celebrate "Flaws":** Identify something you consider a "flaw" and find its beauty. This exercise nurtures your ability to appreciate imperfection.

4. **Create Imperfect Art:** Engage in a creative activity where perfection is not the goal. Embrace the uniqueness of your creation and see it as a reflection of Wabi-Sabi.

5. **Embrace the Passage of Time:** Observe the changes that occur with time, whether it's the aging of objects or the evolving stages of life. Reflect on the beauty of these transformations.

6. **Focus on Essence:** Look beyond appearances to see the essence of things and people. By recognizing inner beauty, you reduce the impact of laziness driven by superficial judgments.

7. **Practice Mindful Presence:** Engage in mindful activities, such as savoring a meal or taking a walk. This practice helps you appreciate the present moment and overcome laziness born from distraction.

In Conclusion:

Wabi-Sabi offers a profound lesson in embracing imperfection and authenticity, acting as a counterbalance to the ideals of perfection that can foster feelings of laziness. By appreciating the beauty in impermanence, the character in flaws, and the authenticity of your journey, you cultivate self-acceptance and purpose. This chapter guides you through the essence of Wabi-

Sabi and provides practical strategies to integrate its principles into your life, helping you overcome the inertia of laziness and celebrate the uniqueness of your existence.

The Paradox of Perfection: How Pursuit of Perfection Leads to Procrastination and Laziness

While the pursuit of perfection may seem like a noble goal, it often leads to unintended consequences, including procrastination and laziness. The desire for flawless outcomes and the fear of making mistakes can create a paralyzing cycle that hinders progress and productivity. Here's how the pursuit of perfection can result in procrastination and laziness:

1. Fear of Failure:
Striving for perfection often comes from a fear of failure or making mistakes. This fear can immobilize you, causing you to delay tasks or avoid them altogether to prevent the possibility of not meeting your own high standards.

2. Overwhelming Expectations:
Setting unrealistically high standards can be overwhelming. When tasks seem insurmountable due to the pressure of perfection, you might procrastinate out of a sense of helplessness or inadequacy.

3. Analysis Paralysis:
The pursuit of perfection can lead to overthinking and overanalyzing every detail. This over-analysis can result in decision-making paralysis, where you delay action due to an inability to choose the "perfect" course of action.

4. Never-Ending Revisions:
Aiming for perfection often leads to endless revisions and adjustments. Constantly refining and fine-tuning can make you feel like you're making progress while actually delaying completion.

5. Lack of Motivation:
The desire for perfection can be mentally draining. As the task becomes associated with immense pressure, your motivation to work on it diminishes, leading to procrastination and laziness.

6. All-or-Nothing Thinking:
Perfectionism often involves an all-or-nothing mindset. If you can't achieve perfection, you might choose to do nothing at all, leading to inaction and laziness.

7. Diminished Confidence:
The relentless pursuit of perfection can erode your self-confidence. When you feel that your efforts are never good enough, you might become demotivated and less inclined to take action.

8. Time-Consuming Details:
Focusing excessively on small details to achieve perfection can consume a disproportionate amount of time. This time investment might lead to neglecting other important tasks, fostering procrastination.

9. Fear of Criticism:
Aiming for perfection can be tied to a fear of criticism or judgment from others. This fear can lead to avoidance of tasks or projects altogether, resulting in laziness.

10. Unrealistic Time Frames:
Striving for perfection can lead to underestimating the time required to complete tasks. When tasks take longer than anticipated, you might postpone or avoid them, succumbing to procrastination.

11. Mental Exhaustion:
The constant pressure to achieve perfection can lead to mental exhaustion. This exhaustion drains your energy and motivation, making laziness more likely.

Breaking the Cycle: Overcoming Perfectionism, Procrastination, and Laziness

Breaking free from the cycle of perfectionism, procrastination, and laziness requires a deliberate and comprehensive approach that addresses the underlying beliefs and behaviors. By adopting a more balanced mindset and incorporating specific strategies, you can effectively navigate these challenges and foster a healthier, more productive way of approaching tasks and goals.

1. Set Realistic Goals and Expectations:
Instead of aiming for flawlessness, set attainable and realistic goals. Break larger tasks into smaller, manageable steps. This approach reduces the overwhelming pressure that perfectionism can create.

2. Accept Mistakes as Learning Opportunities:
Cultivate a mindset that embraces mistakes as valuable learning experiences. Recognize that setbacks and errors are natural steps on the path to improvement and growth.

3. Focus on Progress, Not Perfection:
Shift your focus from achieving perfection to making consistent progress. Celebrate each step forward, regardless of whether it meets an ideal standard.

4. Celebrate Small Wins and Accomplishments:
Acknowledge and celebrate your achievements, no matter how minor they might seem. Positive reinforcement boosts motivation and counters the demotivation of perfectionism.

5. Prioritize Tasks and Set Time Limits:
Create a clear hierarchy of tasks based on importance and urgency. Set realistic time limits for each task to prevent over-investing time due to perfectionist tendencies.

6. Practice Self-Compassion and Mindfulness:

Treat yourself with kindness and understanding, especially when facing challenges or setbacks. Practice mindfulness to stay present and prevent dwelling on perceived imperfections.

7. Embrace Imperfection as Natural:
Internalize the idea that imperfection is a natural and inevitable aspect of life. Accepting imperfections helps reduce the fear of making mistakes and encourages action.

8. Challenge Negative Thought Patterns:
Identify and challenge negative thoughts associated with perfectionism. Replace self-criticism with more balanced and supportive self-talk that encourages action.

9. Break Tasks into Manageable Steps:
Divide tasks into smaller, achievable steps. This approach makes the process less daunting and prevents procrastination stemming from feeling overwhelmed.

10. Experiment with "Good Enough":
Instead of striving for absolute perfection, aim for a level of quality that is "good enough." This approach frees you from excessive perfectionist tendencies.

11. Set a Time Limit for Decision-Making:
Practice setting a specific time limit for making decisions. This prevents overthinking and analysis paralysis that can lead to procrastination.

12. Use the "Two-Minute Rule":
If a task can be completed in two minutes or less, do it immediately. This rule prevents small tasks from piling up and becoming overwhelming.

13. Seek Feedback and External Perspectives:
Share your work with others and seek feedback. External input can provide valuable insights and break the isolation associated with perfectionism.

14. Review and Reflect Regularly:
Set aside time to review your progress and reflect on your achievements. This practice keeps you motivated and helps you adjust your approach as needed.

By recognizing the pitfalls of perfectionism and taking steps to counteract its negative effects, you can break free from the cycle of procrastination and laziness, leading to increased productivity and a healthier mindset.

Examples of How Wabi-Sabi Principles Boost Creativity and Productivity:

1. Innovative Problem Solving:
Embracing imperfection encourages creative problem-solving. Instead of fixating on the "perfect" solution, individuals are more likely to explore unique approaches, leading to innovative solutions that increase productivity.

2. Quick Decision-Making:
Wabi-Sabi's focus on authenticity and imperfection reduces overthinking. People are more likely to make decisions efficiently, allowing them to move forward and complete tasks without getting stuck in analysis paralysis.

3. Reduced Perfectionist Delays:
Embracing the beauty in imperfection helps individuals release the need for everything to be flawless. This reduction in perfectionist tendencies leads to less procrastination and quicker task completion.

4. Flexible Adaptation:
Wabi-Sabi's acknowledgment of impermanence fosters adaptability. When faced with unexpected changes, individuals who embrace these principles are more likely to adapt quickly and find creative solutions, enhancing

productivity.

5. Embracing Mistakes:
Individuals who see beauty in imperfection are more willing to take risks. They embrace mistakes as opportunities for learning and growth, leading to a willingness to experiment and innovate.

6. Authenticity in Creative Work:
Wabi-Sabi encourages artists and creators to infuse their work with authenticity. This leads to more genuine and meaningful creations that resonate with audiences and boost productivity through enhanced engagement.

7. Streamlined Creativity:
Embracing imperfection reduces the pressure to create something flawless. This shift allows creative individuals to focus on the essence of their work, streamlining the creative process and increasing productivity.

8. Efficient Resource Utilization:
Wabi-Sabi principles extend to utilizing available resources. Instead of constantly seeking new materials, individuals embrace reusability and resourcefulness, resulting in more efficient production.

9. Mindful Focus:
The mindfulness inherent in Wabi-Sabi fosters focused attention on the present moment. This mindfulness enhances concentration, reduces distractions, and improves overall productivity.

10. Iterative Improvement:
Wabi-Sabi encourages iterative improvements rather than waiting for perfection. This approach accelerates progress by allowing for continuous adjustments and enhancements.

11. Reduced Performance Anxiety:
The emphasis on authenticity and the recognition of

imperfection reduce performance anxiety. Individuals are more likely to engage in creative endeavors without the fear of judgment, boosting overall productivity.

12. Enhanced Collaboration:
Embracing the uniqueness and authenticity of each team member's contributions fosters collaboration. Teams are more likely to share ideas, experiment, and collectively generate innovative solutions.

13. Efficient Time Management:
Wabi-Sabi principles help individuals distinguish between essential tasks and unnecessary perfectionist tendencies. This clarity leads to improved time management and a focus on high-impact activities.

14. Increased Motivation:
Embracing imperfection reduces the demotivating pressure to achieve unattainable standards. This liberation from perfectionism enhances motivation to create and contribute, leading to increased productivity.

15. Flow State Facilitation:
The mindfulness and authenticity of Wabi-Sabi principles promote the experience of flow—the state of deep concentration and optimal productivity. Flow states are more likely to occur when individuals are fully present and immersed in their work.

By integrating Wabi-Sabi principles into your approach to creativity and productivity, you can experience a transformative shift in how you engage with tasks, embrace imperfection, and leverage authenticity to generate innovative solutions. These principles empower you to overcome perfectionism, reduce procrastination, and create a more productive and fulfilling work environment.

CONCLUSION: EMBRACE THE WISDOM OF JAPANESE TECHNIQUES TO OVERCOME LAZINESS

In this ebook, we embarked on a journey through the rich cultural landscape of Japan, exploring time-tested techniques that combat laziness and inspire a life of purpose, productivity, and growth. Each of these Japanese principles offers a unique perspective on overcoming inertia, harnessing the power of incremental changes, and nurturing an authentic approach to personal and professional pursuits.

Kaizen - Continuous Improvement:
Kaizen encourages us to break down our goals into manageable steps and commit to making small, consistent changes. By embracing this philosophy, we've learned that even the tiniest actions accumulate over time, leading to remarkable progress and combating the stagnation of laziness.

Ikigai - Finding Purpose:

Through the concept of Ikigai, we've explored the profound intersection of passion, mission, vocation, and profession. By aligning our efforts with our Ikigai, we unearth a deep wellspring of motivation that propels us forward, making laziness an afterthought in our pursuit of purpose.

Pomodoro Technique - Time Management:
The Pomodoro Technique introduced us to the power of focused work intervals and structured breaks. By managing our time in this way, we've discovered newfound productivity and concentration, sidestepping the grip of laziness that stems from distraction and fatigue.

Shoshin - Embracing the Beginner's Mind:
We delved into the art of shoshin, learning how to approach tasks with the curiosity and openness of a beginner. By embracing this mindset, we've escaped the trap of multitasking, fostering mindfulness and combating the inefficiency that often accompanies laziness.

Gaman - Perseverance and Endurance:
Gaman unveiled the strength of perseverance and resilience in the face of challenges. By harnessing the power of gaman, we've risen above the allure of laziness, tackling obstacles head-on and forging a path of determined progress.

Kaizen Mindset - Embracing Change:
The Kaizen mindset has guided us in embracing change as a catalyst for growth. By adopting this philosophy, we've shattered the shackles of complacency, adapting to new circumstances, and outpacing the inertia of laziness.

Wabi-Sabi - Embracing Imperfection:
Through Wabi-Sabi, we've learned to find beauty in imperfection and authenticity. By applying these principles, we've liberated ourselves from the unrealistic pursuit of perfection, cultivating self-acceptance and nurturing creativity that transcends the limitations of laziness.

Each of these Japanese techniques offers a unique lens through which to view our lives, tackle challenges, and harness our potential. By incorporating these principles into our daily routines and mindsets, we've embarked on a transformative journey that leads to greater productivity, purpose, and fulfillment. The wisdom of Japan's cultural heritage has illuminated a path that allows us to overcome the inertia of laziness and step into a life characterized by continuous growth, authenticity, and achievement.

Unlocking Your Potential: A Blend of Strategies to Defeat Laziness

As we conclude this journey through the Japanese techniques that empower us to overcome laziness, it's crucial to recognize that conquering inertia requires a holistic approach. Just as a painter blends colors to create a masterpiece, combining these strategies enhances your ability to break free from the grip of laziness and unveil your true potential.

Each technique contributes a unique brushstroke to the canvas of your life. Kaizen's incremental changes, Ikigai's purpose-driven motivation, the Pomodoro Technique's focused bursts, monotasking's mindful immersion, Gaman's unwavering endurance, the Kaizen mindset's adaptable spirit, and Wabi-Sabi's embrace of imperfection—all these strokes form a harmonious whole that paints a vivid portrait of your productivity and well-being.

Taking Action: Transformative Steps to Embrace Change

The true value of these techniques lies in their application. As you close this ebook, consider taking actionable steps to incorporate these principles into your daily routine. Start small, perhaps with the Pomodoro Technique or setting realistic goals inspired by Kaizen. Find your Ikigai and let it light your path. Practice Gaman when faced with challenges, and allow Wabi-Sabi to remind you that authenticity is your strength.

It's not about implementing all these techniques at once. Rather, it's about experimenting, adapting, and discovering what resonates with you. Don't be discouraged by initial setbacks; they're a natural part of growth. With perseverance, you'll navigate the journey toward a more productive, purpose-driven, and fulfilled life.

Optimism: Transforming Your Journey with Positive Impact

As you embark on this transformative journey, remember that the impact of these techniques reaches far beyond mere productivity. They have the potential to enrich your well-being, nourish your creativity, and reshape your approach to challenges. Optimism shines through as you incorporate these strategies, creating a ripple effect that touches not only your personal and professional life but also influences those around you.

With each step, you're rewriting the narrative of your productivity, reclaiming lost time, and embracing the opportunities that unfold. A future filled with accomplishments, authenticity, and personal growth awaits. The path ahead might not always be smooth, but armed with these techniques, you possess the tools to overcome laziness, chart your course, and navigate toward a brighter horizon. The transformation begins now—take those first steps toward a more purposeful and productive existence.

APPENDIX: RESOURCES FOR FURTHER EXPLORATION

Here are some additional resources, recommended readings, and references to delve deeper into the Japanese techniques discussed in this ebook and related topics:

Books:

1. **"One Small Step Can Change Your Life:** The Kaizen Way" by Robert Maurer
2. **"Ikigai: The Japanese Secret to a Long and Happy Life"** by Héctor García and Francesc Miralles
3. **"The Pomodoro Technique"** by Francesco Cirillo
4. **"The One Thing: The Surprisingly Simple Truth Behind Extraordinary Results"** by Gary Keller and Jay Papasan
5. **"Mindful Work: How Meditation Is Changing Business from the Inside Out"** by David Gelles
6. **"Mindset: The New Psychology of Success"** by Carol S. Dweck

Websites and Articles:

1. The Pomodoro Technique Official Website
2. Mindful.org
3. Kaizen Institute

4. TED Talk: "The Art of Stillness" by Pico Iyer

Online Courses and Workshops:

1. **Coursera:** "The Science of Well-Being" by Yale University
2. **Skillshare:** Time Management Techniques
3. **Udemy:** "Mindfulness Meditation: The Science and Practice of Living Fully Present" by Tara Brach

TED Talks:

1. **TED Talk:** "The Power of Vulnerability" by Brené Brown
2. **TED Talk:** "Grit: The Power of Passion and Perseverance" by Angela Lee Duckworth

GLOSSARY OF JAPANESE TERMS

As you navigate the concepts discussed in this ebook, you'll encounter several Japanese terms that hold special significance. To ensure a clear understanding, here's a glossary to familiarize you with these terms:

1. Kaizen (改善):
A Japanese term meaning "continuous improvement." It emphasizes making small, incremental changes over time to achieve meaningful progress.

2. Ikigai (生き甲斐):
The concept of "Ikigai" combines "iki" (life) and "gai" (value) to represent the source of value and purpose in one's life. It refers to the convergence of what you love, what you're good at, what the world needs, and what you can be paid for.

3. Pomodoro Technique (ポモドーロ・テクニック):
A time management method developed by Francesco Cirillo that involves breaking work into focused intervals (usually 25 minutes) followed by short breaks.

4. Shoshin (初心):
The "beginner's mind," embodying the curiosity and openness of a novice. It ushers us to tackle tasks with renewed vigor, sidestepping the clutches of multitasking and inefficiency.

5. Gaman (我慢):

A Japanese term conveying the concept of enduring challenges, adversity, or discomfort with patience, perseverance, and dignity.

6. Kaizen Mindset (改善マインドセット):

The attitude of embracing change, continuous improvement, and adaptability in various aspects of life. It's a mindset that values progress over perfection.

7. Wabi-Sabi (侘寂):

A world-view centered on finding beauty in imperfection, transience, and the natural cycle of growth and decay. It encourages embracing the unique and authentic.

Printed in Great Britain
by Amazon